UNDYING

Michel Faber has written nine other books. In addition to the Whitbread-shortlisted *Under the Skin*, he is the author of the highly acclaimed *The Crimson Petal and the White*, and most recently *The Book of Strange New Things*, which was shortlisted for the Arthur C. Clarke Award and won the Saltire Book of the Year Award 2015. Born in Holland, brought up in Australia, he now lives in the UK. This is his first poetry collection.

UNDYING

A LOVE STORY

MICHEL FABER

CANONGATE

This paperback edition published in 2017 by Canongate
Books

First published in Great Britain in 2016 by
Canongate Books Ltd, 14 High Street, Edinburgh EH1 1TE

www.canongate.co.uk

1

British Library Cataloguing-in-Publication Data
A catalogue record for this book is available on
request from the British Library

ISBN 978 1 78211 856 5

Typeset in Plantin 10/14 pt by Palimpsest Book
Production Ltd, Falkirk, Stirlingshire

Printed and bound in Great Britain by
Clays Ltd, St Ives plc.

Contents

II

Foreword

I used to joke that at the rate I wrote poems, I'd need to live until I was in my nineties before I had enough for a collection. Enough good ones, anyway. The only poem I felt confident to read in public was 'Old Bird, Not Very Well', written in 1999.

Fifteen years later, in June 2014, I was living in Room 212 of Parkside Hospital in London. I'd been living there for several months, camped in a recliner chair next to the bed of my wife Eva. She had multiple myeloma, an incurable cancer of the bone marrow, and was struggling not only with the illness but with the cumulative effects of six years of toxic treatment. Her second stem-cell transplant had failed and her body was a wreck.

Yet we had hopes that a new chemotherapy drug would reverse the latest relapse. With luck, she would get at least six months' remission in which to go home, be reunited with the cats, tidy her affairs, sort through family photographs, maybe go on one last overseas trip to see her sons. I even imagined that she might survive long enough to benefit from new and ever-more-effective myeloma treatments as they were released onto the market in years to come.

It was in that brief period of wishful thinking that – at Eva's suggestion – I read 'Old Bird, Not Very Well' to her oncologist. An optimist, as I suppose oncologists must be, he chose to see it as a poem about living as well as about dying. Eva wasn't convinced. But anyway, poetry had entered that dismal, antiseptic room.

On June 27th, just nine days before Eva's death, when the hope that her plasmacytomas might melt away was fading, I was sitting by her bed as usual. The neuropathy in her hands was so severe that she was unable to use the buzzer to call the nurses, so I was nursing her myself day and night, watching for every movement in the bedclothes, listening out for any murmur. But at this moment she was sleeping peacefully. On Eva's laptop, at the bottom of an untitled Word document I'd been using for all sorts of purposes including a final copyedit of my last novel and drafts of emails to well-wishers, I suddenly wrote two poems, 'Cowboys' and 'Nipples'. Both were alarmingly grim but imbued with whatever it is that poems must have in order to go deeper than the words.

I wrote only those two poems, and then it was time for Eva's cancer to kill her.

Afterwards, as I tried to cope in a world that did not have my dearest friend in it, I wrote more. Sometimes none for several weeks, sometimes five in a day. I hadn't known such need for poetry before. I wish I'd lived into my nineties, with Eva at my side, and never written these things.

Just three of the poems in this collection date from before Eva got sick; two from before I knew her. 'Of Old Age, In Our Sleep' is a recent rewrite of a poem I wrote in the early years of working professionally as a nurse. The original 1984 version was more contrived, showcasing the names of many obscure diseases; a 1996 overhaul was more concise, and the 2014 rewrite simpler still. 'Old People In

Hospital' appears here exactly as I wrote it in 1984, when I was an observer rather than an insider.

The other poems were written throughout 2014 and 2015, and are arranged not in order of their composition but in their appropriate place in the narrative of losing and grieving for Eva.

Michel Faber
Fearn, 2016

Of Old Age, In Our Sleep

Although there is no God, let us not leave off praying;
for words in solemn order may yet prove to be a charm.
Sickness swarms around us, scheming harm,
plotting our ruin behind our back.
Let us pray we may escape attack.

We do not fear to die, to ebb away.
What we fear is endless days
of torture,
forced intimacy
with a body that is not our own;
carnal knowledge
of our cunning abuser, our disease,
who fears no medicine
and hears no pleas.

Let us not leave off praying.
Let us keep our dream close to our heart:
that life is too high-principled
to linger when it should depart.

Yes, let us not leave off praying.
Not for God our soul to keep
but just to die, of old age, in our sleep.

Old Bird, Not Very Well

By the side of the road she stands:
old bird, not very well.
Will she cross? – Yes, perhaps,
in a bit, when the tiredness
passes.

I walk as if on eggshell,
to delay the flit of her wings.
But closer by, step by step, then eye to eye,
I see there will be no such thing.
This bird is waiting
patiently to die.

I am in awe of seeing a bird like this,
standing upright *in extremis*.
We think of birds in two states only:
dead already; death-defying.
Feathered carnage, or still flying.
Finding her, I know I've stumbled
on a moment in a million:
a moment even ornithologists
may never witness:
an old bird, on the point of dying.
Humbled, I intrude on her distress,
her mute, attentive helplessness.

I sit with her a while,
a hundred times her size.
My shoe-heel comes to rest
inches from her breathing breast.

My shadow lassos her personal space:
all that remains of her domain.
Yesterday, the unbounded sky; today
only a fringe of dirt
for massive cars to pass.
One loose feather, scarcely bigger than her eye,
flaps, passive, as they rustle by.
She keeps eerily still,
on the very edge
of no longer being a sparrow.
On the brink
of no longer thinking
birdy thoughts.

Lucky

In late '88, not knowing how lucky I was,
I met a woman who would die of cancer.
I looked into her eyes, and did not see
the dark blood that would fill them when
the platelets were all spent.
All I saw was hazel irises, keen intelligence,
a lick of mascara on the lashes she would lose.
I thrilled to the laugh that pain would quell,
admired the slender neck before it swelled,
and, when she gave herself to me,
I laid my cheek against a cleavage
not yet scarred by venous catheters.
Tenderly I stroked the hair
which was, at that stage, still her own.
I spread her legs, put weight upon her ribcage,
without a worry this might break her bones.
I'd gaze, enchanted, at her naked back, the locus
for the biopsies to come.
Hurrying to meet her in the street,
I'd smile with simple pleasure just to glimpse
my darling who would gladly swallow
pesticide for her future drug regime.
I ran the last few steps to hug her,
squeezing her arms, laying on the pressure,
innocent of the bruises
this might inflict one day.
Hand in hand we walked, and I was proud
to have this destined cancer victim by my side.
I kissed her mouth and tasted only
sweet, untainted Yes.

She was lucky too, back then in '88.
As long as she would live, she loved my body,
ignorant of what it held, and what it holds
in store for me. The skin she fondled
took pity, withheld from her its vilest secrets,
withholds them still (for now),
maintains the smooth façade
on which, on our first night, she shyly laid
her palms, her lips, her breast, her brow.

[indecipherable] kappa

The best doctor in our area
went into the woods one day
and blew his head off.
We were never told
why he did it; his funeral
was in a church, and the papers
were discreet.
A ginger-haired bear of a man,
all Scottish brawn and whiskers,
he liked you. He liked you a lot.
I think he was a little in love with you,
as so many men were.
There was a twinkle in his eye
when he'd bare your thigh
for the pethidine shot
in those halcyon days when migraine
was your big disease.

I wish his rendezvous with you
had pleased him even more.
I wish his ardour had been more profound.
I wish he'd stuck around to be the one
who diagnosed you.
I somehow doubt he would have sent
you home from the local clinic
clutching a scrap of paper scrawled with
[indecipherable] kappa,
immunoglobin [spelling error],
and a tip to go to Google and explore
what 'multiple myeloma' meant.

We followed that prescription
to the letter, sick with terror.
The words, as far as we could tell,
meant death, in agony, and soon.
Which just goes to show
it matters who one's doctor is
on a given afternoon,
and that the best doctor in our area
should perhaps have been on better
medication.

Tests

You tell your children
you're having some tests.
They're familiar with tests.

You tell them
you're having examinations.
They understand examinations.

You say
you're waiting on results.
They know about results.

You are having tests, examinations, waiting
for results, for a piece of paper stating
how you fared.

You're under pressure not to fail.
You are studying survival.
You are ill-prepared.

His Hands Were Shaking

His hands were shaking.
The haematologist
who lifted up your dress
and took the sample from your spine.
Also, he blinks too often.
You want to tell him: Look, this blinking
isn't helping. Either close your eyes
or keep them open.
It would be nice to think
his tremble was distress
at causing pain to one
so beautiful and in her prime,
and not from drink.

In time, when these appointments grow routine,
you'll pray the secretarial roulette
assigns you to a different member of the team.
In time, the trembling blinker will retire,
vanish unannounced and overnight,
and you will never have to sit him down
and say, Hey, listen, I've been thinking
about the shaking and the blinking,
and maybe you and I
are just not right
for each other.

Contraindications

You may experience
necrosis of the jaw, the collapse
of your spine, the disintegration
of your skeleton, ruptures
in the brain, cardiac arrest,
ulcers in the guts, haemorrhaging
sores, embolisms, cataracts . . .

But let's not jump the gun. Relax.
It may never happen!
The following are far more common:
moon face, vomiting, exhaustion,
puffy ankles, night sweats,
rashes, diarrhoea, going bald,
fluid retention, abdominal distension,
'moderate discomfort' (also known as 'pain'),
extremes of hot and cold,
prematurely growing old,
other gripes too numerous to mention.

You may also, if you're vigilant, detect
psychiatric side-effects.
A mood diary may be beneficial.
At certain stages of the cycle
you may find yourself getting tearful
for no apparent reason.

Change Of Life

In our former lives, B.C.,
all sorts of issues seemed to matter –
like minor wastes of money, and a scarcity
of storage space.
Never the canniest shopper,
you'd managed to amass
at least two hundred menstrual pads –
and you were fifty-two.
We did the maths, and made a bet
on whether you would ever get
through all those pricey towelettes.

Now, at fifty-three,
you've started chemotherapy,
and this, in turn, has caused
a swift, ferocious menopause,
or, as our forebears might have said:
'the change of life'.

Suddenly, it's over: the love affair
you once maintained with turtle necks,
mock polo necks, artful layers,
blouses, tailored outfits, fancy collars . . .
Your chest needs air.
A dozen times a day, you grab
the V-necks of your newly-purchased tops
and pull them down, revealing your brassiere.
Panting, you expose your mottled, sweaty flesh.
Our banter shifts: a different tease.
You shameless exhibitionist!

You floozy! Just as well I don't require
a wife who keeps herself demure.
In fact, if you're so hot, my dear,
why not remove the lot?

You stretch beneath me, sexy still,
your clothes cast down next to the drawers
where those superfluous pads are stashed.
We take our time. An hour or more.
Halfway, you briefly, indiscreetly pause
to take a pill.

Prints

Like a pet that comes in wet and muddy,
fur matted with adventure, you return,
bright-eyed and wild, from your nocturnal jaunt.
'Load the pictures in,' you say,
handing me your camera, cold as frost.
You've been haunting Invergordon's shore,
photographing the rigs at Nigg.
I slot the memory card into a USB.
(Your work's all digital now, and done at home.
At hefty cost, you print your own giclées.
You can't be arsed with darkrooms or with labs.
Your trusty Topcon's in a cardboard box somewhere;
You've thrown your dusty chemicals away.)
'Call me when they're in,' you say, and scoot
to the kitchen, footmarks trailing from your boots.

The images are blurry. They were bound to be –
hand-held, no tripod, in the wuthering night.
That's how you want it. Twenty years ago,
you travelled with a swag of gear
and strove to get exposures right.
Now you're chasing arcs of feral light,
smears and shadows, eerie and mysterious.
You're ready to evolve. You're getting serious.

Onscreen, umpteen skies and oil rigs manifest
before us as you sip your drink. You note
the ones that might be worth the paper and the ink.

Then you begin to print. Most likely until dawn.
In your world, Art is never virtual.
It's physical, a thing; it can be held,
you are compelled to make it real.
By morning, there'll be rejects cluttering the floor
and you will ask me which, of several contenders,
is ideal. We'll be agreed. This is 'the one'.
The one which, when you're gone, will bear the seal
of your approval.

If someone, passing by, observed us chatting,
they'd think we're making no big deal of this.
A few prints shifted to one side, an omelette, a kiss.

Right There On The Floor

In our twenty-six years together,
we did some mighty intimate stuff.
But I don't believe we ever
pushed it further than the time
you sat stripped to the waist
on a chair in our bedroom,
me standing behind you
with scissors in my hand,
you looking straight ahead
at the Edinburgh rooftops
saying 'Do it. Just do it.'
And those locks of limp dark hair
that still remained, plastered
to your pale and chemo-blasted skull –
I took them in my fingers, lifted them,
and meticulously
de-sexed you.

Remission

You have achieved zero.
We celebrate with a lunchtime special
at the Thai, on the way home from the hospital.
You order Tom Kha Gai because
your red cell distribution width
is now 15 (as near to normal
as makes no difference).
You choose the crispy fish because
your lymphocytes are 1.6.
The waitress pours your jasmine tea
because your neutrophils are 3.
We pay extra for some greens
because your glomerular filtration rate
is more than 60 ml per minute
(admittedly an estimate).
We share banana fritters because
your albumin is 40 grams per litre.
Brand new hair – ink-black and curly –
springs forth because your creatinine
stands at 69 micromoles.

After dessert, we order coffee.
Let everything settle.
Your paraproteins
are immeasurably small.
You have achieved zero.
Which is to say, the cancer in your marrow
is now so shrunken and discreet
that numbers cannot quantify it.

When it's time to pay,
the waitress brings her gadget,
looks ostentatiously away
as you press the secret buttons.
She tears off the sales receipt,
'For Your Records'. Absent-minded,
you add it to the mulch in your handbag,
too busy re-reading your biochemistry,
coffee stone-cold as you meditate
on phosphates, gamma-glutamyl transferase,
magnesium, calcium, sodium, potassium,
and that momentous zero,
that conditional nothing,
which, after months of eating poison,
you have achieved.

Lebensraum

Your marrow's days are numbered,
your sickly cells condemned,
marked for extermination.
Your body will become
a death chamber
disguised as a woman
quaking under pure white sheets.
Millions of creatures, busily alive,
toil on, oblivious of the monstrous plan.
They'll move as usual through your spine,
your ribs, your pelvis, the pale tunnels
in your legs and arms,
and then a wave of melphalan
(also known as mustard gas)
will douse them with a venom
they can not survive.

Afterwards, when those you hate
are history, your marrow cleansed,
the myriad corpses flushing through your blood,
you'll forge a brave new state
of no immunity.
You'll get your chance
(assuming you are still alive)
to colonise the empty battleground.
A nascent cell community,
fresh from refrigerated exile,
will enter and repopulate
your bones.

You sit in bed, in uniform, prepared.
The toxic swarm's already flowing in you
but has not yet reached its prey.
You eat with normal appetite, knowing
that you have a day, or two, before
you'll be a creature that can eat no more.
Pale and scared, you smile to reassure me.
There's no going back now.
War has been declared.

Since You Last Visited Sopot

Since you last visited Sopot,
a storm swept half the pier into the sea.
The diner where the soup was almost free
(three złoty, with chleb and margarine)
has closed, dumping its coarse clientele
into history. The bag lady of Monte Cassino
has been replaced, it seems, as well.
Now cellphoned tourists, constantly alerted,
chase relaxation in the Baltic sun.
You meet up with your married friends
who are no longer married.
Their brand new partners compliment you
on not looking ill at all, as you eat
fancy schnitzels in the bistro.
A cavern has been dug under the street.
All traffic is diverted. You are having fun.
You stroll around the shops, you try on
shoes, bras, skirts; you buy, buy, buy
like you intend to spend the next ten years
being exquisite. In flux, Poland is in flux,
and nothing's certain, is it?
Everywhere you go, people kiss your cheeks,
plan their futures with you, tell you their secrets,
include you in their dreams, make promises
they will not keep.
Only the marrow of your bone
knows for sure what lies ahead;
only your marrow will keep its vow:

to fell you, to kill you,
to shut you down,
to make you dead.

Reward

London, for you, was the capital
of Claustrophobia.
To get there, you were strapped in a jet,
then tubed underground
for a journey to the centre of your fear:
Marylebone, where you'd bob up briefly
only to sink down again, down, down
into the chamber for your scan.

Burrowed under Bulstrode Place,
Alliance had the best machines
to slice you up with science.
Starved, and dosed with Valium, you'd descend
to the basement where they did the deed.
Kindly staff would lead you blindfolded
into airless realms of ultrasound.
You knew the ropes: the radioactive dye,
the New Age muzak, the high-tech rack,
polystyrene pillows moulded to ensure
you did not bend the flesh laid ready for
the lurid robot eye.

Afterwards, unshackled, you'd be led
back to your little pile of clothes,
and I would help you get back into those.
Still woozy, with your wig skew-whiff,
weird flushes on your face,
you'd waddle to the lift
and say, 'How far are we
from the Hare Krishna place?'

You meant Govinda's restaurant,
your favourite haunt in Soho;
home of the lukewarm thalis,
the mango lassis in the plastic beakers,
the spinach pie in Vishnu's microwave,
the hipsters and the nursing mothers,
faded punks, eternal students,
former carnivores, cooked in righteousness.
Having braved your Sheol
and survived to breathe again,
you wanted papadums, and pronto.
And once you'd had your fill
of karma-free nutrition, and the Valium
was wearing off, you'd say 'How far are we
from the Polish place?'
There, you would scoff real Żurek,
chunks of pig, and pancake for dessert.
You'd lick your fingers – butter, sugar,
maybe coffee froth – and I would reach across
the table and remove, with one sharp tug –
so that it wouldn't hurt –
the cotton-wool ball, specked with blood,
taped to the blackening back of your hand.
Each time a customer came or went,
fresh air would gust into the joint.
Sleepy at last, you'd say: 'God, that was good.
A perfect finish to the day.'

Gifts From Exotic Places

You have a new pal called Rakesh.
You send him photos of Scotland.
He sends you photos of a village
somewhere outside Delhi.
Scotland is beautiful, he opines.
So different, the sunsets.
You show him your paintings, spare him
the challenging ones; he's a regular guy,
prefers landscapes to *memento moris*.
You chat expensively by phone, swap worries
about children. (When you die,
he'll send condolences, call you
'a kind soul', seem genuinely upset.
'It is true,' he'll concede, 'we were having
business relationship and we never met,
but she becomes my good friend.')
Such care Rakesh takes, when filling
your orders. He cuts polystyrene cubes
to fit the empty spaces in between
your packs of Thalimax.
He counts each ersatz Valium,
making sure you get your rupees'-worth.
He smooths potential snags with Customs.
He wraps the packages in muslin.
Seals them with a glob of wax.
You now have enough Thalidomide
to maim three hundred babies.
And Rakesh has photographs
of snow.

Cute

You cannot feel your toes, and so
you walk like a child,
that hint of a toddle,
that newness to bipedal poise.
You would have walked like this, I guess,
in 1960, hand-in-hand with mummy,
fearless in your infancy.
Now your illness has taken fifty years
of confidence off your gait
and made you quite
adorable again.

Beside you, casual and sly,
I keep an eye on your most fetching lack
of balance; the winsome lollop
that might cause a fall.
Half a century back, you'd scrape your knees,
need kisses for your momentary distress,
perhaps get mud stains on your dress.
Today, you might break bones.
Today, your flesh might rend.
Today, something might happen which, in hindsight,
was the omen of your end.

I reach out for your hand.
You walk ahead, oblivious, intent
on the rhythm of your steps,
refreshing your memory
of how this walking trick is done.

One foot in front
of the other one.
Oh, my little girl, how unbearably
cute you have become.

Helpmeet

These were the ways I helped you
in the early days of your ordeal:

Feeling guilty.
Feeling anxious.
Feeling small.
Banging my head, for real, against a wall.
Slamming the handset of a phone so hard
it cracked.
Reminding you that I too
was in pain.
Lamenting all the qualities I lacked.
Exhorting you to flee from me
while you still had the chance
because I was too weak
to bear the strain.

These were my strategies
for coping:

Insomnia.
Pneumonia. Staring at the ceiling.
eBay dealing.
Weeping.
Moping.

After all that, the universe went on.
Your illness had its course to run,
and carried us along, together still,
with life to spare and trials to struggle through –

Essential work for me to do.
Loss by loss, and need by need,
you slipped into my care,
and, act by act, I learned that I was there
for you, and we were in this till the end.
Chore by chore, I earned your trust,
and learned I could be trusted.
My love no longer sought to cure all things,
but went into the warming up of socks,
the whisking of your custard, bowls of soup,
late-night stories, carrying your coat, your purse,
being lover, friend and nurse.
Broken and remade, I was what I had vowed
I could not ever be: your rock.

Such A Simple Thing I Could Have Fixed

We were messpots, the pair of us,
marooned up there in Fearn
and allowed our place to turn
into a hoarders' den,
a car boot sale of things undone.
Unread books clogged up the halls,
unworn jackets faded in the sun,
orphan shoes fell out of shelves,
cupboards bulged with bumf and bric-a-brac
(all to be sorted later, later)
while, in the wardrobes, moths indulged themselves
in wads of knitwear bundled in the back.
Dust bunnies slept under radiators
rarely swept, and almost never mopped.
Magazines grew gently antiquated.
Endless rolls of toilet paper, all half-used,
clothes (unwashed and washed, confused)
lay piled on top of what was once the bed
of a now long-departed child. His ruined
socks remained, and cat puke – vintage, dry –
sat undiscovered in our cosy sty.

We had not always been
so careless, but, when illness came
we went into retreat;
into a space inside our heads
we tried hard to keep neat
while other things degenerated.
Time was short, and we had better things to do
than clean. Instead, we concentrated

on the contents of one room:
me and you.
You read, and wrote, and drew, and waited
for changes, good or evil, in your flesh,
and I would organise your pills
and regularly refresh the linen on your bed.
This much I managed, though the colours
never were co-ordinated –
purple, cream, and several shades of red.

I never asked you if you minded.
Perhaps the colour clashes
caused you pain.
Unmatching bedsheets as you drifted
towards your ultimate lowering
of standards, your loss of all you owned . . .

Such a simple thing I could have
fixed.

Lucencies

Sometimes, the way words sound
is perfect for the thing they name.
Sometimes, to our shame, they let us down.

'Love', for which we should have found
the most melodious breath of air
such as we gave to 'cashmere' or to 'share',
is like a dog's annoying bark, a bore,
'Love! Love! Love! Love!' – until the creature tires
and falls asleep, or we aren't listening anymore.
And as for 'wife' – another canine yelp,
'Wife! Wife! Wife! Wife!' – a yapping whelp
ignored behind a door.
Whoever thought up 'body' for our fleshly form
was plainly not inspired by tenderness or awe.
A dodgy vehicle, this word, comedic, shoddy.

And yet, sometimes, the opposite applies:
horror is wrapped in euphony.
Vicious words that sweetly sing.
What a rich, delicious thing
'myeloma' sounds; a grand indulgence,
this cancer mulling in the bone.
Muted, subtle in its onset,
each darling little cell a 'clone', a harmony
of dark biology, labouring in concert,
its reasoning unknown.
'Death', so soft and moth-like, delicate
as gossamer. And how pretty 'loss' and 'frail';
how dulcet 'chemotherapy' and 'fail'.

Most beautiful of all are those pale glows
revealed by radiography.
'Lucencies'. Surprise! Surprise!
Resembling fireflies,
these ghostly holes embedded in your skull,
your humerus, your pelvis and your spine.
The scans and dyes allow each one to shine.

The Second-Last Time

We never knew
when it would be
the last time.
It was important
not to know.

We made love
the second-last time,
always the second-last time,
as many times
as time allowed.

We'd go to bed
and put our heads
together, trying to find
where you had gone.

Your illness was a vast
terrain, but somehow
again and again
we found you.

Refractory

The killing's done offstage.
On all the websites, no one ever dies
of your disease. They swap advice,
give updates on their holidays,
celebrate anniversaries
of their remissions.
They cheer each other on.
Three thousand musketeers.
Myeloma's on the run.

Then, one by one,
they falter in their flight.
Where do they land?
Why don't we hear from them again?
Why is a search party never sent?
Each time a cancer buddy disappears,
she, or he, winks out without a trace,
and, like the smoothest sleight-of-hand,
a trembling newbie, armed with fears,
a valiant doctor, symptoms, and a treatment plan,
slips in to take their place.

Old People In Hospital

Possessing, of their own,
only a toothbrush and a comb,
like victims of earthquake, fire or flood
fleeing from the threat of death or blood
they've come
for the sanction to go home, restored.
Instead, bored
in their appointed cots they lie
waiting to be cured at last, and die.

Darling Little Dress

On the way
to the hospital today
I saw a darling little dress.
No, not *too* little: just the right
size for you now.
The label says
14
but you know how that can mean
almost anything.
I'd say
it's more like a 12,
but not a *tight* 12.
No, not at all.
Stylish, light and well-designed
in stretchy fabric.
Quite a find.
No, not baggy, not what you would call
a tent. I only meant . . . elasticised.
There is give, that's what I'm saying;
there is give.
The sleeves have cuffs to stow
a tissue in, but otherwise
are loose. But not *too* loose.
Just comfy on your swollen arms.
Not that your arms are
very swollen, just slightly
lacking muscle tone
after the broken bone,
just in need of exercise.

The bosom?
Promising, I think, at first glance.
There's a real chance this might be
nearly optimal.
You'd look shapely; as shapely
as possible
now that you can't wear a bra
anymore, and now your figure
has grown bigger.
The cons? Well, nothing much.
The neckline – I should let you know –
is not as low as you require.
How high? Here, where I touch.
I see you frown, but listen:
this gown, it stretches,
so when the crimson flushes come,
you could simply pull it down.
And at the back? It comes up high,
and I suspect – without seeing it on,
you realise – that it might minimise
the hump that dexamethasone
has dumped in there.
It has no stitches to tear,
no buttons to strain,
no zips to pull in vain.
It would go well with your hair –
no, not the brown you have on now,
another one.
Will it cover your bum? I'm not sure,

that's why I took this picture
for you to study at your leisure.
Yes, I'm aware that all your tights
are threadbare at the rear,
the seams half-perished and worn through,
but I only thought: this dress
would look so beautiful on you
even in bed.

But yes, I must concede, now that we
have the evidence before us,
it does appear quite small.
I could have sworn it said
14, but I agree, it doesn't look it.
Which maybe is the asset of it,
now that your favourite smocks
are on the ample side,
your chemotherapy couture,
your fluid retention range.
This darling little frock
would make a lovely change.

But no, now that you mention it,
I don't believe they had it
in a 16.
It was a one-off,
end-of-season sort of thing,
that I saw on a rail
in a sunny street, not far

from a busy intersection
full of healthy women walking
briskly past this dress
in the opposite direction
from where you are.

Escape Attempts

A tunnel under a prison
dug out with a spoon.
It has been done.
Don't tell me it has not been done.
Let me put your slippers on.
We're going to get you home.
Place one foot on this stair.
One hand on this banister.
Bend at the knee (the stronger one).
Ascend by fifteen centimetres.
It can be done.
It has been done.
Pretend your legs were broken
in an accident, and now
are on the mend.
This is not about cancer.
This is about the Achilles tendon.
This is about the soleus and the tibial nerve.
This is routine convalescence.
This is common physio.
Take my arm, let's go.
Today, two stairs.
Tomorrow, three.
Twenty to get into the plane.
We're going to get you home.
We're going to get you fit.
We'll get you back in shape.
You'll wear clothes of your own
at last, and shoes, real shoes,
and your hair will grow.

It all starts with a single step.
It all depends on how resolutely
you desire escape.
Pretend your legs were broken.
A few stairs and I'll let you sleep.
It'll be easier than it was before,
you'll see. Trust me. Please.
Just take my arm.
Or let me take yours.
Let's get this done.
Don't be
like that.

Nipples

Nipples all over you.
Excited peaks of plasma.
Red, purple, some with areolas.
Your flesh is riotous with the pleasure
of predatory cells.
Each nipple swells
a bit more each day.
I have decided
to watch the one on your foot.
Watch it lovingly
until it flattens
and disappears.
Or until you do.
Whichever happens
first.

Anointed

We are not primitives,
scarifying flesh
with sharpened sticks,
daubing lurid grease
onto the wounds we make,
singing spells by firelight,
praying to deaf gods,
daft and dirty, communal
in our hopeless fight
against a foe we think we know
but do not understand.

No.

We are sophisticates.
We use initiatives.
Everything is fresh.
We inject nothing
that isn't sterile.
You've never slept
in a room so bright.
Never shat yourself
in a bed so clean.
Our specialists speak
the language of your cells.
Have faith, have faith
that they can make you well.

And I? What use am I,
when you're in such good care?

I can dip my fingertips in cream,
reach through the antiseptic air,
straight to the spot where
they've burnt your neck
to scare the cancer back to Hell,
and I can daub the unguent
on your angry skin.

This is not barbarous.
This is science.
This is our way of doing
this thing that we do
to the sick.
We are not thick and superstitious.
We take in clients, and are
benignly, blindly, kindly
vicious.

Ten Tumours On Your Scalp

Reeling from what I had
uncovered,
I washed the blood and sweat
out of your wig.
It came up good as new.
Ready to go back on you.

Switzerland

You tried to phone but
Dignitas was busy.
You begged me, so I wrote instead.
My typing fingers made vibrations
on your bed.
But Switzerland gave no reply.

Or, If Only

It's so easy to die
when you'd really rather not.
The menu of quick demises
is marvellously ample.
You can, for example:
slip on a leaf and break your neck,
be squashed by falling rocks,
be splattered by a train,
be zapped by an electric shock,
burst a vessel in the brain,
sink with a cruise ship,
choke on a fruit pip,
be stung by an exotic mite,
perish in a freak fire,
bleed to death from a bird bite,
be stabbed in someone else's fight,
expire from a hiccup of the heart,
be eaten by an alligator,
be gassed by a faulty radiator,
discover suddenly
that you have a fatal allergy.
This air freshener – 'Magnolia Vanilla' –
issues a stern warning
that solvent abuse can kill
instantly.

How strange, then, that you and I
have so few options open to us.
We'd jump at any offer.
Any speedy death would do us.

Is there no amenable jihadist
who could be persuaded to behead you?
We'd be quite willing to insult Islam
if some resolute young man
could bring his sword to Parkside Hospital
(on the District line to Wimbledon,
then catch the 93 bus).

Or, if only
we could transport you to Westminster,
where armed police stand ready
for terrorists to jump out of the mob.
Your morphine pump – that gizmo squirting dope
into your gut – would make a suspicious bump
if hidden under a shirt. We could hope
it looked enough like a bomb
for the cops to mow you down.
Or, if only
we could buy a ticket to the top
of Tokyo Tower, and smash a window for you.
Or, if only – let's be less ambitious –
you could go to Disneyland, and
unleash yourself from a roller coaster,
fly into the sky of Anaheim or Marne-la-Vallée.
Or, if only you could walk (for goodness' sake,
how simple should this be to organise?)
just a few steps from your bed
into a cab, and from the cab onto a busy motorway,
and, in a wink, be dead.

Instead, we wait.
Each muscle takes its time to lapse.
Each corpuscle spins out its collapse.

We wait for your cells to decay,
one by one.
We wait for each nerve to succumb,
nerve by nerve.
Observe, minute by minute,
millimetre by millimetre,
the tumours take
what they do not deserve.

Another Season

On your bedside cabinet:
a wristwatch with a very quiet tick.
You are too sick to wear it anymore.
It's the old-fashioned kind.
It does not know it is forgotten.
It takes up hardly any space.
Its face points at the window.
It sees the trees in miniature.
You do not see the trees at all.
Spring it was, when you last wore this watch.
Now it is summer, and you do not know.
Your watch is keeping time for you.
When you are ready, its tiny hands
will show they never stopped
being utterly
loyal.

Cowboys

As a child, watching westerns on TV,
I knew cowboys
could be shot and not
die.
They were only dead when
a trickle of blood
appeared at one side
of their mouth,
down to the chin.
That trickle meant
The End.

Now I watch you sleep
and, at the corner of your mouth,
that same dark cedilla.
Together last night we
laboured to clean your teeth.
You with your spastic hands,
me with toothbrush and plastic pick.
Chicken crud between your molars
lodged stubborn as your cancer.
We won
in the end
but fought a little too
hard.

Fluid Balance

I've kept a measure of your sips,
your shuffling visits to the loo,
captured in a blue dish inside the bowl.
The 75 ml of milk
in your corn flakes.
The soup, the custard.
The bags of saline.
The bags of blood.
The platelets, thick as the orange sauce
on the duck you never ate.
I ate it for you.
I drink your water for you, too,
in these last days when
I'm no longer measuring.

Purring

Purring was your favourite sound.
Having slept all night at your feet,
the cat – whichever of our cats was then alive –
would wake up when you finally stirred.
You'd lure him, or her, onto your chest
and the joyful noise would thereupon begin,
released by a tickle under the chin.
How many times have I lain by your side
while your hands caressed sweet-smelling fur,
and the best part of an hour slipped by
as a rapturous mammal purred?

Now that same noise can be heard:
an animal presence, with us, in this room.
All those who enter, listen:
where's it coming from?
That rhythmic, guttural thrum,
that gentle growling in the diaphragm.
It's your lungs: your lungs are purring.
Presumptuous fluid burbles in your breast.
A nurse comes and injects midazolam.
A doctor recommends glycopyrronium.
They're keen for you to die
serenely, like a baby with its lips around
a nipple of morphine. They know what kind
of death is best; they do not like
what's happening to your breath. Their mission
is to stop this bestial sound occurring.
This purring.
This purring.
This purring.

The Time You Chose

It was a smallish space
and we lay close together.
No doubt, to some extent,
we breathed each other's breath.
The angle of my chair
in tandem to your bed
meant that I couldn't see your face,
although I was an arm's length from your head.
I dozed. The hour was late.
You were, I'm almost certain, unaware
that I was even there.
I dozed. You were not dead.
The bedclothes rose and fell.
You were helpless and scary,
like a bear in labour,
like a newborn baby.
For twenty minutes, thirty maybe,
my eyes were closed.
That was the time you chose.

Tight Pullover

In life, you did not relish
being hugged by strange men.

Now, the mortuary van is parked
right near Reception in the dark
at the climax of this hellish night,
and two guys in fancy suits –
one young, one not so young –
are here to rendezvous.

They treat you gently,
undress you with gloved fingers,
roll you on your side,
roll you on your back,
roll you into their arms,
clutch you to their chests.
They shroud you in gauzy white,
wrap you up, immobilise
your limbs, you, who panicked
when caught in a tight pullover.

In minutes they are satisfied.
I have watched but not touched,
impotent to spare you from their grasp.
I thank them, these strange men.
These men you never knew
and did not wish to know.
These men who take you with them
to their van.

F.W. Paine Ltd, Bryson House, Horace Road, Kingston

This is the way it is:
we'll spend the night apart.
I have your new address
on a printed card
but I don't know this city well enough
to picture where you're sleeping.
Besides, it's over now.
I'm surplus to requirements
You are with others of your kind
and I, at last, am absent from your mind.

There are so many people I should tell
that you have left me.
A challenge for another day.
How warm it is! It has become July.
I look up as I walk, and in the sky
I see the first of all the moons
we will not share.

Amateur

The planning of your death
left a lot to be desired.
Right in the middle
of the school vacations.
Most of your teacher friends
vaguely imagined you were
on the mend. Thirty years' worth
of children you had taught
no doubt recalled your kindness,
your good humour, your inspiration,
but thought – as grown-up pupils tend to do –
that you'd vanished from the earth
after their graduation.

Now my internet is down
precisely at the time I must locate
and contact anyone who ever cared.
It's up to me to set a date
for them to come and see you burned.
Some are up for it and others aren't.
Some can travel when others can't.
Some can make it, but only after
you need to vacate
your temporary accommodation.
Some need assistance with their fare.
Some cannot bear to share a space
with current partners of their exes.
Some have a problem
with the absence of religion.
I must negotiate, I must behave with grace.

I'm scared, it's all been left too late, I wish
that we could handle this
together.

You Were Ugly

You were ugly, at the end.
You knew it and I knew it.
Bald, bloated, piggy-eyed,
your flaccid arms bruised black,
your belly mildewed with malignancies,
your vulva and eyelids hairless,
your pupils crossed and sightless,
your breasts weighing down your heartbeat,
your bedbound body seventy-five kilos
of spoiling meat.

Now, choosing photos for your funeral,
I see again how beautiful you were.
How routinely, ravishingly lovely,
how graceful in the flesh,
how happy in your skin.

I called you Gorgeous at the end.
All lovers have names for each other
that are not their names.
Gorgeous was mine for you.
It wasn't true,
in those days before you finally
let yourself go.
You knew it and I knew it.
You were ugly.
But not now.
Not now.

Your Ashes

Your ashes are heavy.
More than I thought.
I carry the shopping bag,
the canister the funeral director
supplied, towards the train
along the main street, cafés, chain stores,
footsore tourists with bags like mine
containing bottles of spirits
lighter than your remains.
I feel like I bought
too much.

You Loved To Dance

In a previous life
in impractical shoes,
you loved to dance.
Sometimes all night,
embraced by sound and light
and maybe by my predecessors:
slinky steppers, snazzy dressers.

Mainly you danced with female friends –
women I would have liked
to invite to your farewell.
I phoned their phantom numbers
gleaned from address books in forgotten drawers.
Google chewed names, chased spoors.
But they could not be found,
these chums who beamed into your face
as you flung your youthful limbs around.
So no one at your funeral ever saw
you in that state of mindless grace,
under a mirror ball, twirling on the floor.

I was no dancer;
you knew that from the start.
My feet securely stowed under the desk,
I databased the avant-garde.
I hated disco, and rejected as grotesque
the party fodder in the charts.
You should have left me to my Art,
put on your high heels and whirled free.
But then, God help you, in mid-spin,

you fell.
Fell hard, for me.

We danced so rarely that I can recall
each time we did it, and to what.
Twice in the mouldy flat where we first met.
Orchestral Manoeuvres In The Dark –
'Dead Girls' – not many couples dance to that.
I played you Severed Heads; you took it
in your stride.
'Those frequencies!' you cried. 'They're uterine!'
German electronica? 'Divine!'
I brought my sounds to where you lived,
out in suburbia, where your neighbours dozed
to Barry Manilow, The Eagles, Fleetwood Mac . . .
I spoiled their barbeques with my cassette
of *Dirtdish* by Wiseblood. You cranked it up,
adored its crude industrial attack. The noise,
to me, was pure aesthetics and, to you, pure sex.
You liked the way I moved in bed
but, looking back, I fret –
Maybe you were less impressed
with how I moved when I was fully dressed.

In 1991, we danced again.
In Hegyeshalom, a hundred miles from Budapest,
dog-tired, our bellies stuffed with palacsinta,
we stood to leave the tavern, suitcases in hand,
but then were serenaded by the band.
They'd asked our country, and misheard

'Australia' as 'Italia', and so
to violin, accordion and goodwill,
we smooched to some old continental ditty.
I showed them how men dance in a big city.
I'm sure they're smirking still.

Come the new millennium,
what with one thing and another,
we danced just one more time:
at our wedding, in a crowd of revellers
assembled in a Polish seaside town.
I did my best to lay my hang-ups down
and shake my tight teetotal ass.
And you know what? It was a blast.
Then ten years passed.
A thousand chances that we didn't take.
And then, when you got ill
the drugs played havoc on your feet;
you stopped responding to the beat.
Our wedding dance would prove our last.

Half a dozen dances in a quarter-century.
I doubt you thought that that was all there'd be.
Frustrated? Bless your heart. You never said.
You made the most of meagre chances.
I wish sometimes you'd had a gigolo,
to take you where I could not go.

I dance sometimes, alone, to Severed Heads.

Rubbing It In

For seventy-five months
I slowed my pace,
a fraction more each week,
to stay in step with you.
At first, I walked more or less
normally, like a healthy man
with a headache or tight shoes.
Incrementally, I cut
the span of my stride,
always maintaining eye contact,
or distracted your attention
to the road ahead,
so you wouldn't notice
what was happening to my tread.

The more chemotherapy you had,
the more I handicapped myself.
At your side, I mimed an easeful motion
while conjuring chains around my feet.
We moved, eventually, like the Myeloma Twins.
We tortoised to the outskirts of the room,
climbed the distant summit of the stairs,
voyaged to the far end of the street.
Towards the end, when I would inch with you
to the Ultima Thule of the hospital loo,
I'd ceased to pretend.

Today, I jumped on a mountain bike
and cycled eight miles, to get something done,
goddamn it, in a hurry.

It was easy.
A shameful lapse of tact.
Flaunting the fact
that I don't have what you've got.
Forcing you to swallow
that I'm alive
and you're not.

Restraining Order

Unshaven, shabby and unwashed,
I haunt the place where we last slept
together, and refuse to leave.
Why no one calls the cops to move
me on, I do not understand.
Surely someone will lay a hand
on my clammy shoulder, and say
'Nothing more to see.'

In the beginning, all that love
was awfully romantic in its way,
but now the novelty's worn thin
and normalcy is overdue.
This loyalty to what's dead and gone,
this clinging to what's no longer
mine; it's borderline obsessed.
Give it a rest.

A polite suggestion, buddy:
Give her some space. Steer clear
of where you think she ought to be.
She won't be there. Instead, why not
give some thought to personal hygiene.
Adopt a healthier diet. Keep well-hydrated.
Find other topics of conversation.
Maybe join a group of folk like you,
to talk things through.
By all means take some time
to grieve, but don't let it become

excessive. Accept the situation:
you've lost her. Try not to be
possessive.

Account Holder

The helpline man
refuses to help
because I am not you.
He needs – by letter – proof
that you are dead, he needs
to see your name and your disease
and the date your suffering ended
so that our bills can be amended
to be mine instead, all mine,
and then and only then
will the helpline men
let me go ahead
and wait in the queue
and listen, listen, listen,
holding on for that hush
when the music stops
and a voice, at last, will ask
how they can be
of assistance.

Don't Hesitate To Ask

So many of the people I've
informed that she is dead
have said
'If there's anything
we can do, anything at all,
don't hesitate to ask.'

Well,
actually,
since you offer,
yes:
Would you mind driving me
headlong through the universe
at ten million miles an hour,
scattering stars like trashcans
scorching the sky?
Put your foot to the floor,
crash right through the gate of Fate,
trespass galaxies, straight over
black holes and supernovas
to the hideout of God.
Wait for me while I break
down the boardroom door
and drag the high and mighty fucker
out of his conference with Eternity,
his summit on the Mysteries Of Life,
and get him to explain to me
why it was so necessary
to torture and humiliate

and finally exterminate
my wife.

But no.
These things I do not say
because I know
that by 'anything at all'
you mean
a cup of tea
or a lift into town,
if you're going
that way
anyway.

They Say

They say –
they who have done this grieving thing
before me –
they say, in time, the sharp recall
of horrors fades away, leaving
room for gentler, happier, further-distant
glows of reminiscence.
Others say –
I will forget your face.

Bring the years on.
Watch this space.

Please Leave All Baggage On Board

Bewildered, meek, I lift my magazine
to let the hostess check I'm safely clasped.
Around her neck, the sleek transparent tube
of an oxygen mask, so similar to an IV line.
Her life jacket's just for Show And Tell;
her spiel about emergencies has passed
unnoticed in our massive metal shell. Sit tight,
and once we have permission we'll be on our way.
Enjoy this flight. Tomorrow we'll be in the USA.

The plane crawls forward, picks up speed, and then
heaves off the ground. This is the moment when
we'd take each other's hand, and gently squeeze:
another journey formally begun. Seated at my side,
a stranger with vermilion claws.
Her gaze implores the crew. They make her wait.
Oh, how she longs to medicate herself with wine.
Much later, in the ghostly light, she'll lay
her lacquered hair against my arm
and sleep, consoled at last, as, by remote control,
this raft of bodies is dispatched towards its goal.

The Sorrento Hotel Invites You To Help Conserve Water

I leave this hotel room the way I found it;
the bed so neat and spotless, it's as though
nobody slept here, nothing happened, and instead
the guest just paced around it, fully dressed
and, at the shrouded window, sat and traced
the slow disintegration of the view.
The maids will love me: all they'll need to do
is smooth the sheets a little, set the pillow straight,
replace a plastic trinket of shampoo.

But late last night, if you'd been here with me,
after we'd talked about the food, the town,
the petty details of the day, and laid
our jetlagged bodies down to rest, I guarantee
we would have turned to face each other
and, in a heartbeat, been each other's lover
and this huge bed, this monument of kitsch
would have been joyously unmade,
the pillows crushed, the quilt pulled down,
the blankets pitched onto the floor,
the sheets all churned and christened
with our smell.
And, in the morning, cleaning personnel would wheel
their trolley in, survey the scene, and understand
this bedroom held a woman and her man.

Wake-up call. You're dead another day.
The hotel hopes I have enjoyed my stay.

Dolmades

My stroll in Central Park
was safely unremarkable. It rained,
the children never ventured from their homes,
the autumn colours gloomed to monochrome.
The birds were just like any birds you'd seen
a thousand times before, the squirrels
standard issue, and the dogs
constrained by their indentured walkers,
heads down, trained, routine.
Nothing to move you, nothing to spark
a flash of rapture, and no scene of pathos
to provide you with a fruture reverie.
Nothing gained, if you'd been lent another year
to come here on this New York trip with me.

The subway – always full of risk
of some transcendent incident,
some spate of oddness to provoke
your love of people – played it cool,
stayed untransporting, free of wild event.
Just trains and passengers,
brisk and destination-bent.
OK, there was that busker, pitched at 59th,
right near the exit, wet, and blowing
'Raindrops Keep Fallin'' on the clarinet.
But on your scale of one to ten
I bet he would have scored a two, a three at most –
too slick, too low on poignancy, too knowing
to plant in you a fond 'Remember when . . .?'

More good luck: none of my hosts
have cats. No mogs to bring you to your knees
with helpless, let-me-be-your-mum desire
Unless I count the pictures – thumbnail glows –
displayed by Maya, on her phone,
of absent Ollie posing in her other home.
But no, I think this sight would not have made
a deep impression; you'd have praised him, I
    suppose,
but then forgotten fast
this gadget glimpse, not meant to last.

And so my first adventure, after you, goes on.
Before I know it, I've survived this city,
shaken hands, attended dinners, struck no one
as a pathetic wreck; I've laughed; been witty,
never once collapsed, or been undone
by grief, by pity, by regret.
Incredible how, on the taxi ride
to catch my onward flight,
life pulls out all the stops to spare me pain.
The driver's nice, but has a spiel
to which you would have been immune, I feel.
In any case, had you been there, you might
have snoozed (as you so often did in cars)
and missed his anecdotes about the mayor
who gave LaGuardia its name.
I'm sure you'd not have thanked your stars
you came.
Not looked at me and squeezed my hand

84

as if to say 'How lovely that my life contained
this precious moment too!'

Now, at the airport, I relax.
I've made it, I've escaped intact.
Security's all smiles, they wave me through,
they let me keep my razor, I retrieve my shoes,
my wallet, keys, I'm good to go.
Perhaps, now that I'm nowhere that I know,
four thousand miles from where I lost you,
I will find that distance tricks the mind
and leaves the longing stranded in a far-off place.
Look: I'm moving on
to the departure lounge, where I will wait,
dog-tired, at my appointed gate,
penned in a space so soulless even you
would see no merit in it. No, come on, admit it:
it's just as well you didn't make it.
You're better off not being here.

To fill the empty minutes till it's time,
I stand perusing airport food – the usual fare:
banana muffins, bagels, sandwiches in cellophane,
expensive flavoured water, nuts.
But then, defences down, I'm
skewered in the guts.
There, on a tray, in a glassed-in display,
dolmades.
Vine leaves.
Dozens of them.

The real deal, plump and crudely-shapen,
sweating olive oil, lasciviously green.
Your eyes light up, I hear your voice,
excited, child-like, at this great surprise.
You want dolmades, you'd forgotten how
consumingly you loved them.
'Oh, can we get some? Please?'

You did not speak, and I did not reply.
An hour remains until they let me fly.
You are here with me, silently
wanting, hoping, yearning, thirsting,
craving, lusting, pining, waiting.
I do not buy dolmades.
I do not buy
dolmades.

My First Date After You

(For Ann Patty)

In a restaurant, I wait
for a woman.
My first date
after you.
I know that she and I will kiss,
embrace, make approving noises
about the weather,
assess the damage to our faces,
the weight we've failed to lose
these ten years since
our previous get-together.
She arrives, slightly late,
and we do all of the above.

After lunch, we take a walk
in the sunshine without you,
enjoying New York.
I have no shame in my agenda:
to pump her for memories;
to talk about you.
That's all I want from everyone,
everywhere I go:
to talk about you,
to venerate our love.

Now, reflecting on those hours I spent,
in the restaurant and in the park,

I draw a blank. What did she say?
Bless her, she forgave my scant attention
to her life, accepted that her job was just to mention
all she was able to retrieve about my wife.
She did her best, I've reason to believe –
but not a word has stuck.
The over-bright sun: I remember that.
Her devilish grin, undimmed by age.
Handing her the photo of you, in bed
with her dog. (That dog, she said, is still alive.)
Hard as I strive, I can't remember more.
Holy fuck –
You died just eighty days before,
and I was in no state
for that first date.

You Chose So Well

I walk into the flat you chose for us,
and the way the sunlight falls
on the tangerine walls, the nooks and alcoves
and the uncollected mail,
makes me want to tell you,
You chose well.

The sixty-two stairs
were the sole drawback, a bridge
to be crossed when we were old.
The light and space up there
was worth the climb.
So, in the meantime:
Sold.

A few years in,
you had to stop halfway
to gather oxygen.
On those grey steps, you got stabbed
in the legs
by delinquent veins.
After your transplant, I placed
a chair on each landing, rungs on the ladder
up to the bedroom shadowed
by treetops, circled by seagulls.

Towards the end, your sojourns here grew
scarce; your blood preferred
the ground floor B&B, and later
the clinic with its elevator.

A tenant took the room where you once perched
contented at the window, looking down
on streetlife in the lamplit night.

And now, I enter our domain, unfazed
by those sixty-two steps, dazed by the colours.
You chose them and I painted them.
Our bed still overlooks the chimneytops.
The light still casts its spell.
My love, you chose so well.

Risotto

You bought too many wigs.
All that luxurious soft hair,
slightly second-hand,
in boxes.
Too sad to keep.
Too intimate to sell.
Too valuable to throw away.
What am I supposed to do?

You bought too many clothes.
So many multiples of the same
cancer-friendly tops,
oedema-friendly tights,
myopathy-friendly socks,
accident-friendly undies,
nighties you never even wore
and hated
in a range of colours.

You accumulated
too many phones too many pairs of glasses too many
emery boards too many nail clippers too many
lip salves too many battery chargers too many
toothpicks too many cameras too many
kohl sticks too many shoes mouthwashes razors
combs odd socks bottles of Boots No.7
unlabelled keys to God knows what locks
in what places I will never be again
if indeed I was ever there.

You always cooked too much food.
Loads of leftovers went into the freezer
for another day, except that on another day
you cooked afresh, and again too much.
Today I took out your last risotto
and savoured every swallow,
every grain of what was once
a storage problem,
and how I wish there was enough
for more.

Your Plants

Hey, listen:
can I let your plants die?
I never knew their names,
where they came from, or how high
they were supposed to grow,
how dry their veins could stand to go.
They've loitered in the bathroom like
shabby derelicts, unshiftable and frail,
waiting without hope for passersby
to take pity.
I am the water man.
I am the man with the water.
I am the man who stands in the shower,
twenty inches from those plants,
weeping into the torrent,
all that liquid plenty down the plughole
while your plants, brown and stoic,
watch.

Hey, listen:
I never asked for them.
I never promised anything.
I made no pledge to nurse those leaves, those buds,
those mad green shoots on the parched stumps,
those silent thankyous for a cupful of attention
sloshed into their cobwebby soil
three weeks ago, or was it
five?
I never said I'd keep your plants alive.

The Tower

'As far as the tower,' you'd say
in those days when you could still walk
by my side, on the path to Balanroich.
The tower, a skeletal Eiffel, full of electricity,
marked the limit of your energy.
You'd set off from our house, rugged-up
against the elements. The breeze tugged at
your wig, your raincoat was too big,
your faithful sheepskin boots hugged
your poor unfeeling feet.
'As far as the tower,' you'd say.
It was, at most, three hundred yards away.
Once upon a time, you'd barely notice
such a distance, in your haste to move.
But in those last two years
you only wished to prove
the wheelchair was not always
necessary.

Today, alone, in spring, I take the air
that you no longer breathe.
Unfit, overweight, I'm still in better shape
than you were when you walked with me.
I pause beside the tower, gauge its height,
Squint against the morning light.
Birds flit around in pairs, the trees show off
their leaves, encouraged by the sun.
A plastic bag over my head, and half a dozen
morphine ampoules past their Use-By date
should be enough, I think.

I will not go as far
as chemotherapy, I swear.
No one can make me go there.
I have – you know damn well – my reasons.
I'll be the master of my destiny.
Who knows? The cancer that's reserved for me
may even be a kind that lets me climb
this tower, beyond the barbed wire,
beyond the highest branches
of the trees you loved to see.
Spring. Spring. Blur of green.
How you savoured all these birches.
You kept track of their progress through the seasons
and, latterly, they marked your waning power.
'As far as that tree.'
'As far as that bend in the path.'
'As far as the tower.'

Do Not Launder Or Dry Clean, Do Not Use With Helpless Person, Infant Or Person Insensitive To Heat, No Serviceable Parts Inside

One of our electric blankets
has become passive-aggressive;
it threatens indolently
to kill me.
We kept them going 24/7, year in year out,
to give the cats a treat, or just
in case we felt like making love.
Now mine has had enough.
Most of it has stopped working; one corner
under my shoulder and another under my shin
are lightbulb-hot. Each morning, I wonder
if I'm imagining it. I stroke my palms
where I have lain, note the coolness
right next to the heat. Eventually
I lift the sheet, lift the suspect, and find
a faint scorch on the mattress,
an embryonic blush of burn
on the surface of a forty-kilo block
of flammable stuffing.

I do nothing.
I continue, nightly, to braise
my shoulder and my calf.
What sweet rescue if a stroke
of electricity dispatched me in my sleep.
What blessed relief if this whole room
were consumed in flames and smoke.

My very own, home-made
crematorium.

Weeks pass. I compromise.
I switch the blanket off when
I'm not lying on it; I concede
it would be a shame to stand outside and watch
our house burn down with all your things in it.
In fact, I grow a bit obsessive-compulsive:
Keys, wallet, have I switched off the blanket?
But still, each night, I lay me down to
tempt fate. In time, I can even feel
the hidden pattern of the wires.

At last, good sense prevails.
I pull the hazard off the mattress,
throw it in the trash, and, with my hands, admit
that you will not be coming back
to your side of this bed; I shift
your electric blanket an arm's length to the right,
and for the first time since you went into the furnace
your space is cold at night.

My body lies safe now, with just a thin sheet
between me and the thing that kept you snug.
Just a thin sheet
between me and your menstrual blood,
me and the marks
we made together.

Proliferation

Your inbox is riddled with it.
Your system overrun
with matter that's no use to anyone.

When you were alive, real humans
sometimes emailed you.
Those days are gone.
Your friends know better.
Now only algorithms chatter.
It's been a long time, Eva, they remark.

I hesitate to call this spam.
Solicited, the bulk of it.
CancerCompass Newsletter.
Oncology Daily Digest.
Leukemia Alert.
You had so many hours of dark
to fill, while I retired to get my rest.
By day, we talked of literature and cats;
by night, you crunched the stats.

The march of science goes on.
CancerNetwork has a slideshow.
eChemist has a sale that ends at five.
Take action Eva, make your choice.
LAST CHANCE, EVA, for free delivery.
This Week In Oncology is pleased to announce
a brand new paper on tumour metastasis.
Dial-in at 5pm Eastern Time to ask a question LIVE
about high-risk myeloma and its prognosis.

So many words I didn't know were even words,
like 'apoptosis', 'atresia', 'intravasation' . . .
Your inbox pullulates with this stuff.
The senders have no way of knowing
you have had enough.

Barley Fields, Fearn, 16 August, 8 O'Clock

The light is how you like it:
stealthy in its beauty.
Dusk is scheduled in ten minutes;
shadows queue to do their duty.
Our window view is dulling down
with nothing special in it.

But no: beyond the house, beyond the trees,
beyond the shadows' limits,
the fields are joyous and absurdly bold,
each bale of straw a block of gold,
the mile-high stubble drenched in dayglow,
the sun imbued in everything.
This was the yellow that you flew
ten thousand miles to stalk.
This was the yellow that you captured
on your tripod-laden walks so many years ago,
in prints of Cibachrome;
this landscape with light to burn,
this place you vowed would be your home.

And now they're here again.
See! In plain view and illicit
as always, for ten minutes only.
Slip some shoes on and run!
Let's go see the show.
Let's photograph the sun.
Blink and you'll miss it.

Put your shoes on.
Put your shoes on.
The light is how you like it.
Where on earth are you? I have gathered
all your shoes together, and the night
must fall
on time.

Kodachrome (b. 1935 – d. 2009)

The borrowed slide projector comes
with a screen bigger than me,
heavy, rolled up in itself, a monster,
like my sorrow.
I decide to let it lie
untouched. I wait for night
and activate the clump of Bakelite
(it works! it whirrs! it groans with age!)
and shine a square of pallid light
straight from the ancient lens
onto the couch, the wall, a sketchbook page,
and finally, the best solution:
a canvas of pure, woven white,
a painting that you never made.

Here, on that blankness that you meant to fill,
I see your adolescent self, frozen, still.
In the backyard where your dolls were burned,
behind the house where your mum was bashed,
and holes were kicked in plasterboard
and prayers were offered to the Lord
(none of which these slides archive),
you stand, unknowable, alive.

Here's you with cat held to your chest
(the breasts I loved are yet to sprout).
Here's you with husband number one
when you were courting, goofy, blessed
by the Jehovah's Witnesses,
snapped outside the Kingdom Hall.

How big his teeth, how small his eyes!
How thick your glasses, and how ill-advised
your hairstyle, tweedy jacket, dress.
The time since then has showed he would remain
himself, but older and more beetle-browed.
You, at first so plain, grew gorgeous with the years
and, by the time we met, attained your best.
We flourished after Kodachrome.
No slides preserve our happiness.

It ought to be enough, this glimpse,
on empty canvas in this empty home.
This gadget can be borrowed more than once,
and I can see again your foreign face,
your awkward, unfamiliar grin.
The slide itself takes up no space.
And yet, I feel this image is on loan;
I want to own, to access, to possess.
I get you focused on the canvas plane
and, with my camera, click you through
onto the memory card within.

I shut the old projector down.
Its motor lapses, comatose.
I coil the cords, I cap the lens,
I stow the plastic carousels
and sheathe in styrene moulds the ends
of this unwieldy piece of kit.
Fit it back into its box.

No closure, and that cat you cuddled?
Gone, the canvas white and pure,
poised on the sofa where you do not sit
in the house where you no longer live
in a world where you are nothing more
than an exposure, bits
of pixel and emulsion,
invisible and safely stored.
Your lost past.
My forlorn compulsion.

Trying It On

I have this fantasy.
It has the flimsy, dreamy logic
of a porn flick.
An unknown woman turns up at my house,
knocks on the door. She needs
no explanation. I lead her
straight into the bedroom.
She unzips her coat. Another knock.
Another woman. And another.
Knock. Knock. Knock.
With the merest nod, they enter.
A dozen women, all not unlike you.
Your height, your build. Your waist,
your thighs, there's even one who's got
that same concavity between her breasts.
They file into our bedroom;
stand waiting for my signal
for the action to commence.

I swing the wardrobe open wide.
Your favourite clothes, a little musty now,
are crammed inside.
The women coo.
The nearest says: 'That skirt.'
'That silky top: the one in blue.'
The woman with your legs strips to her panties,
pulls on your jeans. They're a perfect fit.
Another woman's trying on a shirt.
Your ochre camisole does wonders

for the girl who's shaped
like you were in your curvy forties.
She'll need a darker bra, though, than her own.
No problem. Somewhere on these shelves –
'That hand-sewn dress, oh God, if you only knew
how long I've searched –'
'That knitted poncho with the turtleneck –'
'Help me: this one fastens at the back –'

The orgy lasts for minutes, hours, who can tell?
A dozen females pleasuring themselves.
Your wardrobe empties, every jacket, every shawl.
Each garment bears the traces of your skin,
and mine, because I loved the way you dressed,
and let you know, with my caress.

Our Cats No Longer Miss You

After not much time at all,
the animals' vigil
at the windowsill
stops.
Your voice is a flavour of food
no longer brought home
from the shops.
You fail to mark your territory.
All spaces are vacancies.

Your smell goes stale
and is replaced by soap, by dirt,
by microwave emissions.
These are the new conditions:
bowls in fewer rooms,
no sounds of laughter,
one less hump under the duvet,
lights switched on before dawn,
less chance of tidbits from the table,
mediocre stroking.

The young one curries favour
with the neighbours.
The old one
gets sick and dies.
Eleven months is a big chunk
of a cat's allotted span.
She suffers, in the end.
A friend who came to your funeral
digs the hole.

It's only small.
The body, cradled in my hands,
is scarcely bigger
than your head.

Tamarind

Today I found a use for tamarind.
You'd bought a pot of it, never got around to it.
It sat there, sealed, ignored in favour
of your more familiar standbys – coriander,
cumin, garlic, ginger, cancer.
I've been going through our cupboards.
So many things are past their date.
They won't kill me. I call their bluff.
You would have liked the trout I baked tonight.
Tamarind is splendid stuff.

I'm cleaning up this house.
I'm cooking for myself. I'm losing weight.
Recipe by recipe, I rid shelf after shelf
of dried-out mushrooms. Jalapeño peppers,
Blue Dragon corn cobs (rusty lid).
Dusty egg noodles (Medium) stacked in piles.
Powdered soup you bought in a Polish sklep
in Shepherd's Bush with wheelchair aisles.
Ancient coconut milk. Nine rices.
Bizarrely-shaped pastas. Yellow lentils,
five bags full. A jar of pickled figs.
Well, no, the figs went in the bin.
I cannot find a use for everything.

I'm restoring order. I'm on the case.
Taking charge. Let me show you how.
I'm not impulsive, wasteful, not like you.
Nothing new will come into this place
until I've worked through all that is here now.

So many freedoms I can claim!
See this vintage chutney? Don't tell me
it has possibilities. Into the trash it goes.
And while we're at it: the junk beneath the sink,
the rubbish in the boiler room. Who needs
a broken torch? A mouldy pair of gloves?
The manual for a long-defunct machine?
Stand aside, woman, and watch me clean.
I make a judgement call on these old tubes of paint:
they'll never be unscrewed again.
This vase is cracked. I toss it.
Don't complain. What made you think
we'd ever spread this fertiliser in the garden?
Grass grows regardless and, I'm sorry, but
we really have too many towels,
and too much medicine for your bowels.
I'll never read your self-help books.
They've done what good they're going to do.
Bid them adieu.
Stay silent. Utter not a peep
defending all these things I cannot keep.
I'll determine what should still be left behind.
I'll sort through all your files, and at last
give each of them a memorable name.
Names that you could actually find!
You'll thank me
when I'm done.
Just try to keep in mind,
as you stare from the wings, aghast
at all the things I've binned:

I've spared you the shame
of once having wasted £1.99
on tamarind.

The 13th

The first snowflakes fall.
Thoughtless, weightless,
they've come from nothing
to line the world, to make the known
unknown, to bring ephemeral change
to all that was familiar.
A million of them, soft and merciless,
remake the landscape in their image.

Each year we saw them come.
Each year, we knew we'd be here when
they'd gone.
Solid as the landscape, you
enjoyed their fleeting reign.
They surrendered, melting, on your breast,
bright twinkles on the wool that kept you warm,
specks of wetness in your hair.
Your boots crushed them underfoot,
your camera froze them in time,
long after they had vanished.

Now it's you who's bodiless.
So tentatively there,
so insubstantial in the air
that the snowflakes fall right through you.
Now it's you who's powerless –
beautiful as you are –
to stay.

The Moment Of Capture

I wake, befuddled. I am not alone.
There's a body in my bedroom that is not my own.
Breathing soft, so near to where I lie.
Slim, petite and graceful, this guy is on his knees
beside my luggage,
fingers deep inside.
Our eyes meet. In my fog of sleep, I fail
to comprehend how we came to be
together. Wide-eyed, he speaks to me
in French, I struggle to translate,
he rises to his dainty feet, turns tail.
Too late, I spring up from my bed.

I cruise the streets of Brussels, poke my head
in each café that's serving *déjeuner*
in case I spot the thieving little scum.
What's French for 'camera'? *Appareil?*
Cette appareil – contene – images de ma femme –
Ma femme est morte –
Retournez – maintenant – s'il vous plaît.

I get no chance to try my little spiel:
that camera's gone for good.
(You in the sheepskin boots and furry hood:
that was one. You in the garden: another.)
I return to base. My hosts regret my loss.
A fellow guest forgot to lock the door.
This neighbourhood is thick with thieves.
Such things have happened here before.

Shall I speak to Belgium's police?
Describe my nondescript *voleur*?
Describe the camera I lost?
I don't recall its make, its model or its cost.
All I remember is you,
on a bright day in the Highlands,
holding still for me
in the moment of capture,
and that mechanical whirr
as the gadget promised us
this was forever.

Clarification

Nine months after your funeral,
I finally track him down:
your first husband.
He was present at an earlier ceremony,
wedded in The Truth, guiding your hand
to sign his name and make it half your own.
Faux-leather album, slightly mildewed,
photos unglued and slipping free
in the bottom drawer of seventies debris.
I offer scans or copies; he declines.
I doubt he would have flown
twelve thousand miles to see
you boxed and ready for disposal.

By email, he is generous with his time.
Four decades on, for no one's benefit but mine,
he leads me to the wreckage of your marriage.
For you, it was a girlhood tale
that you had long since ceased to tell.
For him, it's ancient history as well.
For me, it's gaps I need to fill.
Greedy for his memories, I'm grateful
as he feeds me morsels of your past.
Your ears are surely burning.

Safely faceless, he and I
perform a most peculiar dance
of forthrightness and tact.
Husband to husband, kept separate
by continents and fate, we span

a windblown wire across your silent space.
Weighing each word, I ask to be set straight.
He's in a different time-zone, so I wait.
Each day I fear the answer will be no.
Yet still we meet halfway.
Me and this other man you lost,
this man you thought no longer loved you.
What a shame that I can't let you know
this is, in point of fact,
not so.

Well, We Made It

Two old dears get on the train.
They must be eighty, might be ninety,
married more than half a century.
He with hearing-aid and oatmeal cardigan,
his flesh all bone and Adam's apple.
She with translucent skin, birdclaw-thin –
breast cancer survivor, could well be,
or just an elderly gamine.
Briefly breathless,
they locate their reservations
and, once settled, calm their respirations.
Having won a dozen battles
in the war with tickets, toilets, turnstiles,
heavy luggage, narrow aisles, overpasses,
tricky schedules read with the wrong glasses,
they reward themselves with ScotRail tea
and a shortbread, shaped for two.
The old man unlips his gnarly grin,
leans forward, asks his wife,
'Are you OK?'
She smiles.

My love, had you not died
but lived another twenty, thirty years,
these two old dears might have been us.
Me, farting, manful as I lift your case
up to where such things must go.
You sparse-haired, blue-veined,
a remnant of the beauty you once were.

Fellow-travellers even so.
How sweet – as sweet as shortbread on my tongue –
to earn the pity of the young.

Inverurie, 30 May 2015

Unfamiliar road
through landscape after rain,
freshly revealed, hyper-real,
and, on a hilltop, noble and absurd,
a rusted metal whatnot
that looks just like an animal.
How you would have crowed!
Mirth brings you back to life
in that moment before the sight
is buried under rising earth.

Anniversary

When your cancer's sniper cells
had scored direct hits on your legs, your arms,
your feet, your hands, your neck, your thighs,
their next objective was your eyes.
The ambush must have happened in the night,
while you were sleeping. I observed
the aftermath. Your pupils, weakened and estranged.
The TV, bolted to the wall on the far side
of the room, was suddenly beyond your range,
the news reduced to faceless voices
and a flickering blur.

I railed against the cruelty of this change.
This punishment was undeserved.
Muscle by muscle, you'd been robbed
of all that might have lent you courage
to endure.

Meanwhile, on the screen above us,
civil war in Syria, life on planet Earth.
Though you could barely see,
you knew those shapes were countless refugees.
'I'm just one person,' you reminded me.
'Each of those Syrians has an equal worth.
They want to live, they've lost their home, they're
    scared.'

Fuck the Syrians, I almost said.
There's gross unfairness in this room!

But it was not my right to voice your rage.
And twelve days later, you were dead.

A year has passed since then, and there's no sign
that justice has the faintest chance to thrive.
Last month, a bigot slaughtered worshippers
in a church in Carolina, leaving only four alive.
Last week, in Tunisia, a crowd of pensioners
were murdered as they drowsed on holiday.
Today's the anniversary – not just of our tragedy,
but of London's bombing, 7 July 2005.

What can I do to mark the passing of my wife?
Your cancer killed you and yet not one person
thought to call the BBC.
No weeping passersby left wreaths outside the scene,
no hacks accused the government
of being slow to act.
Your illness, with its crises flagging every stage,
failed, even so, to win a Wikipedia page.
In global terms, yours was an insignificant life.
Your death a negligible fact.

All I can do, in what remains of my brief time,
is mention, to whoever cares to listen,
that a woman once existed, who was kind
and beautiful and brave, and I will not forget
how the world was altered, beyond recognition,
when we met.

Come To Bed

That last year or so
we seldom slept together.
There were three of us in our marriage.
You, me, and your cancer.

I would come and see
how the two of you were getting on.
If you fancied some breakfast
after a long night together.
Some lunch after a lie-in,
some supper after dusk
as the curtains were drawing in.
Later still, I would read to you.
Bedtime stories.
On bad days, all time was bedtime.
Then I would retire
to let you fail to sleep.

You had your routine.
Your stash of tissues under the pillow,
your unsleeping pills,
your immobile phone,
your thin white scarf, your thicker pink one,
your writing pads, your pens just there.
Everything in reach
but me.

Now I lie in the bed that came from Australia.
Old when I bought it, in a charity shop,
this mattress loved our bodies, grateful

as a Rescue pet, set for the long haul.
We shipped it ten thousand miles,
berthed it in your Highland paradise,
braced our naked feet against its base
countless times, man, bed and wife.
This bed has doubled now in size
and I am single, huddled, blanketed in harm.
I am in danger of forgetting
the feel of your fingers,
the warmth of your belly against my back,
the shape of your thigh under my palm.
In danger of losing you
forever to the other room.

I have waited patiently, oh so patiently,
before asking
in my gentlest voice:
Can I lure you away?
Can I tempt you with our history?
This mattress has missed you.
Hollowed, it is fit for no one else.
Oh, I know you are snug
in your self-containment.
I know you are settled,
finally at ease
in your ash.
But please . . .
Just for tonight . . .
Just for one night . . .
Sleep with me.

Lucencies (2)

You worked covertly,
nurturing by stealth.
You lifted people up,
nudged them to transcend
their limitations,
in sickness and in health.
Those you assisted looked around
to thank you, but you'd hide.
When your influence began to spread
too far, you died. I still hear
your whisper in my ear:
'Let's be going.'

If I could scan this planet
with X-rays that detect the presence
of your timely interventions,
I'm sure I'd find them
in places you would not expect.
You're dead. I know. And it is not for me
to show you death is not the end.
But you left lucencies of grace
secreted in the world,
still glowing.